LOST YEOVIL

BOB OSBORN

AMBERLEY

To Carolyn and Alice

First published 2020

Amberley Publishing
The Hill, Stroud
Gloucestershire, GL5 4EP

www.amberley-books.com

Copyright © Bob Osborn, 2020

British Library Cataloguing in Publication Data.

A catalogue record for this book is available from the British Library.

ISBN 978 1 4456 9364 4 (print)
ISBN 978 1 4456 9365 1 (ebook)

Origination by Amberley Publishing.
Printed in the UK.

Contents

A horse-drawn ice cream van visits Sandringham Road during the 1960s.

Introduction

This sepia-toned photograph looking east along Middle Street dates to around 1875.

In common with most towns across the United Kingdom, Yeovil has always seen constant change. Within living memory, the Glovers' Walk precinct development of the 1960s and the Quedam Shopping Centre development of the 1980s saw the face of the town centre lost forever – much to the chagrin of many Yeovilians. When these developments are seen in combination with the major road schemes of recent years, such as converting both Kingston and Reckleford to dual carriageway status and the construction of Queensway, more and more of 'old' Yeovil seems to have been lost.

However much we may rue the loss of what we consider Yeovil's essential character, it should be remembered that these recent changes are only the latest in a series of what might be termed 'ongoing developments' that have taken place throughout the centuries. Early Yeovil was chiefly comprised of wooden buildings with thatched roofs, built close together and fire spreading from one burning property to its neighbours was a constant threat. Catastrophic fires, all, in turn, labelled the 'Great Fire of Yeovil', broke out in 1620, 1640 and again in 1643 when many properties in the town were destroyed. In fact, the destruction caused by the 'Great Fire' of 28 July 1640 was so serious that a 'Protection' was issued by Charles I authorising a nationwide 'collection' for Yeovil as a result of this disastrous fire. The collection was not made on the authority of letters from the Privy Council but was granted by letters patent, a type of legal instrument in the form of a published written order issued by the monarch. In the year 1449 117 houses in Yeovil (around a quarter of the entire town) had been destroyed by an earlier 'Great Fire'.

In 1856 Daniel Vickery recorded, 'Perhaps, however, no part of the borough has undergone more changes in appearance and reality – dwellings and dwellers – than what is popularly called The Borough. Not long since the site of Mr Dingley's shop was covered by one of the old wood and plaster buildings, and that of the Wilts and Dorset Bank by a block of low mean dwellings.'

Even in 1890, the date of this postcard, Middle Street was incredibly narrow.

Street widening, undertaken to cope with an ever-growing volume of traffic, is another major cause of loss of buildings and changing streetscapes. Yet again, this is nothing new. Middle Street, for example, had been widened piecemeal through the centuries. Edward Bullock Watts' map of Middle Street of 1829 shows that it varied in width from as little as 10 feet 5 inches (3.8 metres) at a point between Bond Street and the Triangle, 11 feet 6 inches (3.5 metres) outside the Castle Inn, opposite Union Street, and 12 feet 4 inches (3.76 metres) outside the George Inn. The street was 24 feet 6 inches (7.47 metres) at its widest part, by Bond Street. Indeed, the map also shows a dotted line being a proposed new frontage for several buildings on the north side of Middle Street between Bond Street and the Triangle.

In 1835 a major fire destroyed the King's Arms in Silver Street along with several other premises. Following the fire, all the premises from the Kings Arms to the Pall Tavern were rebuilt further back from the road so that Silver Street could be widened, thereby easing congestion in the centre of the town.

These then, together with the individual replacement of buildings, have been the major influences on the changing face of Yeovil. This book attempts to capture, through old photographs, some of the character of 'lost Yeovil'. As well as lost street scenes and individual lost buildings, the book also looks at lost building interiors and a number of trades once familiar around the town, but now lost to time.

Looking east along Middle Street in 1895. It remained this narrow until the 1970s.

Lost Street Scenes

Middle Street, looking west towards the Borough, in 1930.

Above and opposite: The earliest known depiction of High Street, this drawing shows the Fleur-de-Lys next door to Yeovil's first post office (replaced in 1836 by Linsey Denner's shop). The sketch has been dated to between 1766 and 1780 based on notes on its back referring to the people depicted. The Fleur-de-Lys building itself is constructed in red brick with stone quoins, string course, window surrounds and the fine columned entrance. The windows are of the sash type to the front elevation but a casement window is open on the gable indicating one or more rooms in the roof space. At ground level, the two grilled windows at pavement level indicate an extensive cellar.

Opposite is a part of a hand-tinted stone lithograph, entitled 'Market Place – Yeovil' by Henry Burn (1807–84). There are not many known stone lithographs by Henry Burn because he left for Australia in 1852. It was published by William Porter and Henry Marsh Custard in Yeovil during January 1839 and printed by Charles Joseph Hullmandel of London.

The tree on the left marks the location of today's King George Street and the building to its right may have been the original George Inn. The large three-storey building with the two-storey projecting bay and a hanging sign was the King's Head Inn. It was known before the mid-seventeenth century as the Cock in the Hoop. Next is the china and glassware establishment of George Glyde. The building on the right, a property belonging to the Corporation, was the chemist and druggist premises of Edward Granger. Both before and after this lithograph, this building was the Fleur-de-Lys (seen above), today it survives (albeit altered) as part of Beales' store.

This is a very early photograph by William Barrett (half of a stereoscopic pair) dating to around 1860, looking across the Borough to High Street. The bank building on the right, which still stands, was less than ten years old at the time, and the Town Hall, left of centre, was around fifteen years old. Today, none of the buildings on the left survive.

This photograph, of around 1865, looks to the Borough from High Street. Of the buildings either side of Middle Street, London House (to the left) was demolished in 1913 for the present bank building and the Medical Hall (to the right) was destroyed by enemy bombing in 1941. The blur at the bottom left is a person who moved while the photograph was being taken.

A hand-coloured and heavily touched-up photograph of High Street dating to 1907. If you look closely you will see that most of the people have no shadows, and were added to the photograph in the photographer's studio. All the buildings on the left have since disappeared and the tree marks the location of today's King George Street.

At one time many Yeovil roads were paved with hard-wearing granite setts (often erroneously called cobbles, which are rounded). The example here, now sadly covered in tarmac, is in Coldharbour Lane (which runs behind South Western Terrace) and was the original track to Coldharbour Farm. The farmhouse was demolished for Yeovil Town station in the late 1850s.

On the left, London House was built in 1836 and, for most of its existence of just seventy-eight years, it was occupied by a succession of drapers. It was demolished in 1913 and the present building, built for the Midland Bank, opened in 1914. On the right and seen below, the Medical Hall was built in 1860 and the *Sherborne Mercury* noted: 'Those who remember the low range of buildings which formerly stood there, can scarcely realise the imposing edifice which has now taken its place.'

The Medical Hall was bombed and completely destroyed late in the evening of Good Friday, 11 April 1941. It was rebuilt by Boots the Chemist after the war and the present building opened in 1956. The building at right was William Maynard's shop and restaurant in the Borough. Before Maynard's premises were built, the site was occupied by a medieval building known as The Bow. Maynard's later became the Cadena Restaurant and was itself demolished in 1983.

This photograph is of Middle Street looking east, as seen in 1871. None of these buildings survive today. The medieval George Inn, on the right, was demolished in 1962 for street widening but most of the other buildings were demolished in the late nineteenth or early twentieth century because they were substandard even for that time.

Middle Street, Yeovil

This postcard of 1918 looks west along Middle Street with the Borough in the background. By this time the plaster covering the George Inn had been removed, exposing the structural timberwork. While the buildings on the right are, generally, the same today, all the buildings on the left have been replaced.

Again looking west towards the Borough, this sepia-toned photograph of around 1905 clearly shows the severe narrowing of Middle Street by the George Inn – bearing in mind, of course, that this was the main road from London to the West Country at the time. This was the narrowest choke point until the 1970s, although there had been narrower places a hundred years earlier.

This photograph dates to the 1930s and looks east along Middle Street from a point just west of Bond Street. The New Inn, just right of centre with the large projecting sign, is on the corner of Bond Street and today is Nationwide's premises. Most of the other buildings in this view disappeared during the 1940s and 1950s.

Lower Middle Street photographed around 1890 and looking east from the Triangle. Thomas Jesty's furniture emporium is at the extreme right and immediately beyond it are the short front gardens of Ebenezer Terrace. In the distance are the triple-gabled offices of the gasworks (recently premises of St Margaret's Hospice). On the extreme left, the cottage with a small front garden was soon to be demolished and replaced with the block of shops surmounted by a series of four small domes seen in the photograph below.

The shops at the extreme right, with the cupolas and awnings, remained until the 1960s. Below, this 1930s postcard looks back to the Triangle from Lower Middle Street. The large building on the right is the Coronation Hotel & Vaults, which opened in 1905. All the buildings on the right of this postcard were demolished in the 1960s when the Glovers' Walk shopping centre was built.

The houses seen here in 1983 were the first to be built along the south side of Townsend (that part of Lower Middle Street between Wyndham Street and the junction with Reckleford/Sherborne Road) and are seen on Edward Bullock Watts' map of 1831. Below, the western end of the run of buildings on the south side of Townsend are photographed in the early 1980s.

To the right of Dave's Plaice fish and chip shop (earlier called the Fish Fryer) is the Duke of Wellington and Cashman's Shopping Centre. All the buildings in both of these photographs were demolished around 1992.

This photograph, taken around 1905, looks north along Kingston towards Fiveways, and shows just how narrow and winding Kingston was before it was straightened and converted to a dual carriageway. The Red Lion Inn is seen on the right, partly hidden by the tree that marked the corner of Bide's Gardens. Next door to the pub, identified by the flagpole, was the Yeovil County School. Every building in this photograph was demolished.

This almost aerial view along Kingston looks south-east from the upper floor of Swallowcliffe House. The photograph was taken in the 1950s when Swallowcliffe House was used as the Ministry of Labour Employment Exchange. In the foreground, to the right of centre, are Kingston Villas – rare survivors of the widening of Kingston. The large white gable wall just beyond Kingston Villas belongs to Kingston House, later part of the Park School. To the lower left is the entrance gateway in the garden wall of the Unitarian chapel.

This view looks north along single-carriageway Kingston from close to its junction with Reckleford. It was photographed in 1956 by Yeovil photographer H.A. 'Jack' Cooper. The Kingston Hotel had been built in the 1850s as a private residence known as Pitney Villa but didn't become a hotel until the early 1960s. It eventually absorbed the three-storey houses alongside. On the right is the Red Lion Hotel and the tree on the extreme right marked the corner of Bide's Gardens.

This is probably one of the last photographs of these Kingston buildings. From, and including, the Kingston Hotel (on the far left) until almost as far as the Duke of York (off photo to the right), every building was soon to be demolished for the building of Queensway, the new dual carriageway bisecting the town from Hendford to Kingston. The road layout would also alter around this roundabout.

By 1973, the date of this photograph, Kingston had become a dual carriageway. The new Kingston/Reckleford/Princes Street roundabout lies in front of the houses in the previous photograph. All these buildings would be demolished for the new Queensway.

On the right, the Kingston Hotel and the buildings to the north (running off photo to the right) have now been demolished. Works have also begun to redesign the Kingston/Reckleford/Princes Street roundabout. Top left is Vincent's car showroom (now Batten's offices) on the corner of Court Ash and Princes Street, while opposite Haine's the butcher's premises survived destruction.

This photograph shows the construction of the pedestrian underpass beneath Kingston. On the right is the new District Hospital, opened in 1973. The left half of the photograph shows, compared with previous photographs, just how many buildings were demolished in Kingston for the road widening and the building of the new hospital.

Cottages on Reckleford, by Goldcroft, photographed in the early 1960s. The cottages were demolished soon after this photograph was taken. In the 1840s all the cottages were owned by bright smith (silversmith) George Rendell, who rented them out. One of them was later the grocery and bakery of Henry C. Tomkins. On the far right is the Nautilus Works on the opposite corner of Goldcroft.

Demolition began on the nurses' accommodation blocks facing Higher Kingston during the summer of 2014 in order to create a car park for hospital visitors. This accommodation block, on the corner of Higher Kingston (left) and Roping Road (right), is ready for demolition. The main District Hospital building is opposite, off photo to the left.

This photograph, taken in December 2014 from an upper floor of the District Hospital, looks across Higher Kingston towards the new car park that replaced the nurses' accommodation blocks of the photograph above. I wonder how many people realised the new car park would all be dug up by May 2016 for the new multistorey car park for hospital visitors?

This late 1980s view looks east from Huish towards Westminster Street and features an unusual view of Douglas Seaton's garage, car showrooms and petrol filling station. Built on a site of 100,000 square feet that had previously been Petter's iron foundry, the new premises were floodlit at night. The building, with its iconic tower, opened in 1931 but was demolished in 1991.

This view looks east, along Huish, in 1977. Just a few years later, this view was totally changed with the construction of Queensway, which cut right across the centre of this scene. The two shops on the left, now converted to houses, remain today. All the other buildings, including Huish Junior School on the extreme right, were demolished for the building of the new dual carriageway.

This photograph was taken in 1986 and, again, looks west along Huish. By this time the new Queensway dual carriageway had bisected western Yeovil, including Huish, and in this photograph it is depicted by the fence running across the road in the distance. Huish Junior School, left of centre, survives at this time but would be demolished in 1991 and the site is now the Tesco filling station. The gap between the Huish National School, on the right, and the irregular block of shops and houses at the centre was the entrance area to the football ground.

Continuing south from Huish, this is a view from the southern end of Salthouse Lane looking towards West Hendford. The buildings are Yeovil's first ambulance station, later used by the St John's Ambulance. The site is now a block of flats.

Vicarage Street had been a street within the medieval town of Yeovil since Saxon times. The street itself ran eastwards from Silver Street, opposite St John's Church, before veering south-east and joining Middle Street at Vennell's Cross, now known as the Triangle. At one time it was almost entirely residential and these cottages, photographed in 1958, were the last remnants of domestic architecture in the street. These buildings were demolished shortly after the photograph was taken, and the site was cleared for a car park (seen below).

This is a view that will bring back memories for many older Yeovilians. The car park, along with the rest of Vicarage Street, disappeared in the 1980s with the construction of the Quedam Shopping Centre. Today, only the Methodist church survives from this 1980s streetscape.

Looking from the eastern end of Vicarage Street, this view of the Triangle and Lower Middle Street is from a postcard of around 1944. Note the underground toilets at right, at this time with black and white markings painted on so that traffic would stand a better chance of seeing it in the blackout. The malodorous lavatories were closed, completely dug up and the hole filled in during August 1971.

This photograph, of the mid-1960s, shows the buildings at the western end of Vicarage Street. At the far end, the single-storey building was for many years a fire engine house, which later became part of Denning Brothers butcher's shop in Silver Street (demolished in the 1980s). The large two-storey building dominating this photograph was the former premises of the small engineering company Harbour & Hobbs.

This photograph dates to around 1920 and shows the western end of Vicarage Street as seen from Silver Street. On the left corner was the butcher's shop owned by the Parker family, and on the right corner was the Denning Brothers' butcher's shop. The cottages seen in the centre were demolished shortly after this photograph was taken and Percy Winsor erected a new building for his agricultural machinery business. None of these buildings survive today.

Dating to the early 1980s, this photograph was taken from the Vicarage Street car park (featured in the previous page spread). It looks beyond Vicarage Street, obscured by the low stone wall but running across the lower part of the photograph, to Vincent Street. The buildings in the far distance, at the point where Vincent Street turned left and Vincent Place was to the right, are the only buildings that survive today.

Above is a closer view of the shops and houses on the western side of Vincent Street, taken in 1983. The shops included Tartan Cleaners, Shumend, War on Want and Mervyn's hairdressers. Beyond the shops, the street becomes residential. Once again, none of these buildings escaped demolition.

This photograph shows Vincent Street looking towards Vicarage Street from its northern end. Taken only weeks after the photo above, the houses are now all empty and being prepared for demolition. Indeed, in the foreground, it is seen that the northern side of Earle Street has already been demolished. Within weeks all the buildings in both of these photographs were demolished.

This 1955 aerial photograph shows much of the area that would disappear with the building of the 1980s Quedam Shopping Centre. Running across the bottom is Middle Street, joined by Vicarage Street, coming in from above and left, at the centre. Running across the centre of the photograph is Earle Street, which joins Vincent Street (in dark shade) at right angles. Vincent Street runs towards the three rows of terraced housing towards the top left corner. Vincent Street continues to the left, while Vincent Place continues to the right. The two upper terraces are Cecil Street and Salisbury Terrace on Reckleford.

This view looks south from the 90° bend in Vincent Street. The northern houses of Earle Street have already been demolished and a car park made on the site on the left. The white building on the corner of Earle Street and Vincent Street would soon be demolished. On the right, Vincent Street runs south to join Vicarage Street.

This photograph was taken in 1983 from the southern end of Vincent Street after works had begun for the Quedam Shopping Centre. On the extreme right, the Albion Inn has almost been completely demolished. The photograph looks across Vicarage Street to what had been the car park, with the backs of Middle Street buildings in the background and Frederick Place in the centre.

These cottages are in Sparrow Road. Photographed in 1956, the camera looks west towards Mudford Road. The cottages, typical of Yeovil, were built in local Yeovil stone that was affected by heat from fires – hence the flues often had to be rebuilt in brickwork as seen on the end house here.

Photographed in the 1950s, South Street is seen from the Petters Way car park, at this time used as the Friday market. On the extreme left is the end wall of the Three Choughs, the white house right of centre was the market toll collector's house owned by the Corporation and on the right is the old Cheese Market, from 1913 used as the town fire station. The domed turret on the far right is on the roof of the municipal offices in King George Street.

A 1960s photograph showing glove manufacturer Thomas Fooks' house (on the right) in its South Street setting. The white building on the left with two people outside is on the corner of Bond Street, while on the opposite side is just seen the junction with Park Street. The house seen on the corner of South Street and Park Street was Park Street House, the home of Fooks' son, William.

Looking east, this view of South Street, closer to the Triangle, dates to around 1920. The three-storey white building at the centre was William Fooks' glove factory while the garden wall on the extreme right was the South Street entrance to Park Street House. The building on the right with a shopfront and the Pitman's School sign was originally the Park Street House gardener's cottage.

Move on sixty years and this is the same view in 1997. The cottages on the left have gone and the site is now a car park. Beyond, the old Methodist chapel is about to be demolished. The Pitman's School building survives on the right, but beyond it, the glove factory has been replaced by the Box Company buildings. The chapel, Pitman's School building and the box factory have all since disappeared.

The name Horsey Lane derives the Horsey family who were Stewards of Yeovil under the Abbess of Syon, Lord of Yeovil, from 1415 when Henry V granted Yeovil to the abbey after his victory over the French at Agincourt. Originally Horsey Lane, sometimes referred to as Horses Lane, ran from its entrance opposite the Three Choughs in Hendford to the catchpool (now the junction of West Hendford and Beer Street) before turning sharply left to Hendford Bridge by today's Railway Hotel.

Belmont Street was built between 1886 and 1901 in a field to the south of Mill Lane called Mill Close. It was constructed as a cul-de-sac off Addlewell Lane and ran adjacent to, and parallel with, Mill Lane. The area was demolished in 1987, the date of this photograph, for the development of Central Acre and the extension of Summerhouse Terrace to join what remained of Park Street.

Summerhouse Terrace was originally a short road, built just after 1880, between Stars Lane and Mill Lane. Today, of course, it has been extended east beyond Stars Lane to become Old Station Road and west beyond Mill Lane to become Park Street. On the 1901 and 1912 Ordnance Surveys the land to the south of Summerhouse Terrace, later the conglomeration of small factories and workshops seen here, was shown as 'Allotment Gardens'. Even until the 1960s Summerhouse Terrace ended at Mill Lane.

Here, Lysander Road is seen as a single-lane road running across the top of this 1980s photograph, with part of the Westland's complex at the top. The bottom of the photograph is dominated by the large gasholder which, in the 1950s, stood alone in a field. By the time of this photograph the Forest Hill estate completely surrounded it. The gasholder was removed in the 1980s.

Felix Place was constructed during the 1840s and named after Felix Curtis, who owned the land on which it was built. Felix Place connected Huish and West Hendford to the east of the Crown public house – seen here at the centre. A short terrace of houses ran parallel to the main Felix Place dwellings immediately behind the Crown. Felix Place was demolished in the early 1960s and the site is now under the western end of Tesco's southern car park.

Wellington Street was named after the Duke of Wellington (1769–1852), the hero of the 1815 Battle of Waterloo and Prime Minister of England between 1828 and 1830. Wellington Street probably dates from the time of Wellington's premiership as it was not shown on Watt's map of 1806 but it was built on a field called Waterloo Gardens, named as such after the 1815 battle had taken place. Wellington Street, seen here from Huish in the 1960s, was completely demolished around 1968 to make way for the new Wellington Flats housing development.

This 1960s photograph looks east along West Hendford towards its junction with Hendford, opposite the Three Choughs, and shows just how narrow West Hendford was at its eastern end. The cottages on the left were all demolished in the 1960s. All along the right-hand side are the former livery stables and, later, garaging of the Three Choughs Hotel, some parts were demolished and replaced with a block of flats. The large building on the right is now part of the Manor Hotel's accommodation.

The earliest mention of today's Market Street in the records occurs in a document of 1355 in which it was referred to as Ford Street, simply because it had a ford across a small stream. The small brook was called the Rackel or Rackle and was little more than an open sewer. It crossed the road close to the Pall Tavern and was shallow enough to be forded, hence the early name of Market Street for hundreds of years was Rackleford, or Reckleford – right up until the 1840s. Most of these houses were demolished in the 1960s shortly after this photograph was taken.

Here, Brunswick Street is seen from Hendford and photographed in the 1960s. The houses on the left were demolished and now form a grassy bank opposite the entrance to Goldenstones. On the right is Nichols' Tannery, specialising in processing lambskins and suede. In 1825 'the new road belonging to Peter Daniell' was combined with Park Street running from the east and replaced the circuitous and somewhat steep route of Addlewell Lane and Chant's Path. Originally, the new road was known as New France, then France Street and finally Brunswick Street.

A wintry scene of the snow-covered houses of Park Street on the flanks of Penn Hill and overlooking the passing goods train on its way to Taunton in the 1950s. Originally known as Frogg Lane or Frogg Street, Park Street was laid out and built by Peter Daniell between 1825 and 1834 along the edge of his Penn House estate. It ran from its junction with South Street in a southerly direction around the flank of Penn Hill. All these houses were demolished in the 1960s.

This photograph, taken in 2006, shows the demolition of the Reckleford premises of the 'Cooker King' Alan Lovell between Wyndham Street and Sherborne Road. However, Alan was much better known as the 'Lion Man of Yeovil' because, prior to the Dangerous Wild Animals Act 1976, he kept Tara, a fully grown, one-eyed lioness at the rear of the premises (he also had a camel called Jasmine). Alan and Tara often raised money for charity.

Photographed in September 2016, this image looks west along Sherborne Road from the junction with Lyde Road (on the right), before this junction was changed forever with a new layout and traffic lights. The grassy area in the foreground, now gone, was the last vestige of a field called Great Meadway (Meadway was the original name of Lyde Road), and was itself a remnant of the great medieval East Field of Kingston Manor.

This photograph was taken in the 1960s and looks west along Preston Road and the road running off to the right is Willow Road. The three-bay house end-on to Preston Road with a corner shop in its left-hand side is Providence Cottage. The building on the right was originally a leather tannery but converted into a flour mill known as Newis' Mills. Both cottage and mills were demolished shortly after this photograph was taken.

This photograph looks west along Preston Road during the 1960s. The thatched cottages (Nos 214 and 216 Preston Road) were demolished for street widening shortly after the photograph was taken. The large house whose roof is glimpsed behind the cottages was Sutherland House, home to Yeovil poet and author Walter Raymond from around 1892 to 1905. The tower on the left is that of St James' Church, Preston Plucknett.

Lost Buildings

The iconic tower of Douglas Seaton's garage, on the corner of Huish and Clarence Street, was demolished in 1991.

By the middle of the nineteenth century the old Tolle Hall, which had served as an early town hall, was in a bad state of repair and was deemed inadequate for the growing town. Consequently, a new combined Town Hall and Market was built, opening in 1849. That the new Town Hall, seen here at centre with its clock tower in the late 1920s, was completely out of scale and character to the existing streetscape didn't really matter to the Victorians, provided it showed off the leading townspeople's aspirations towards grandeur. The building was destroyed by fire in 1935.

This photograph of Hendford, probably taken in the 1960s, shows how narrow South Street (with the car driving out of it) was at the time. The Three Choughs Hotel is on the the far left. Chudleigh's Seed Merchants was demolished in the 1960s to widen South Street. It is most likely that this was Charles Dodge's premises when he was listed as 'Corn & General Merchants of Hendford' in Collins' Yeovil Directory of 1907. The building next to it (with the BSA signs) had earlier been the photographic studios of John Chaffin and then his son between 1862 and 1919.

By the time of this 2002 photograph, the former stables and garage of the Three Choughs Hotel, on the corner between Hendford and West Hendford, had been converted to a nightclub. Initially, it was called the Camelot Suite in the early 1970s, then Oliver's in the late 1970s and the Electric Studios, or simply the Studios, in the early 1980s. By its final closing in 2003 it was called Arena.

The Oxford Inn was originally cottages at the junction of Waterloo Lane, running north, and West Hendford, running west. In 1845 the Town Commissioners proposed converting the Oxford Inn into a Watch House and Superintendent's house but the plans came to nothing. The Oxford Inn stopped trading in the late 1940s, and later became the offices of the Petter & Warren architectural practice, before being demolished in the early 1970s.

Thomas Cave began brewing in Yeovil in the 1830s. By 1854, Joseph Brutton had moved to Yeovil and entered into business with Cave, and from that date the business was known as Cave & Brutton, later Brutton & Co. after Cave's death. The new malthouse, featured at the centre of this 1980s photograph, was one of the first pneumatic malting houses in the country and was built by 1885. The Yeovil Brewery ceased to brew in 1965 and the site of the malthouse is now covered by Tesco's car park.

Seen here in a photograph of the 1980s, Edwin Snell's printing works was on the corner of Park Road and Clarence Street. Edwin Snell later moved to Babylon Hill and the printing works were subsequently occupied by Haynes publishing company before becoming the Gardens nightclub in 1981 and the First Floor Gym. The building was demolished around 2008 and was replaced by a block of flats.

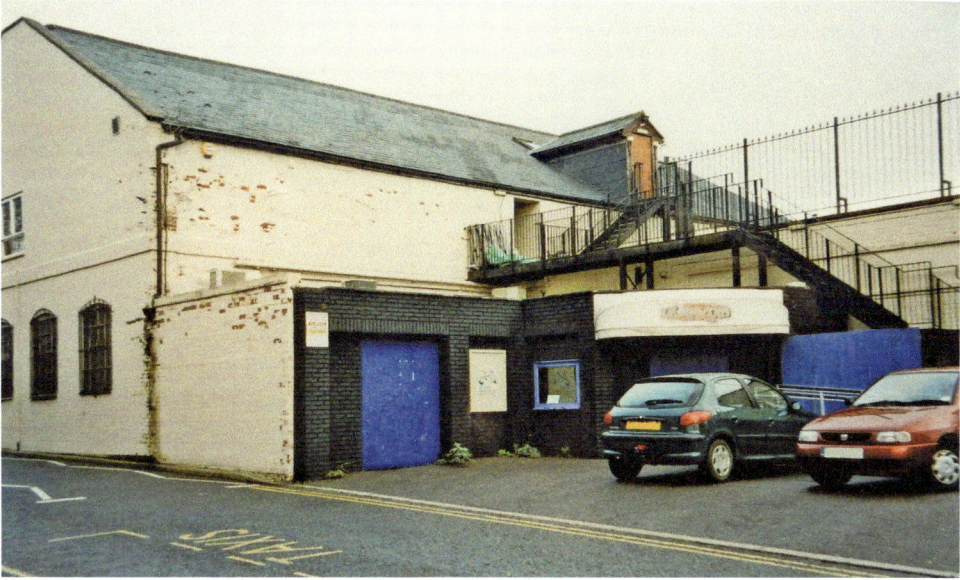

Photographed in 2006, this was the Clarence Street entrance to the Gardens Nightclub and Restaurant. Although by this time renamed 'Le Jardin', it had been one of Yeovil's trendier nightspots of the early 1990s and featured plastic palm trees placed around the edge of the dance floor. It gradually became less trendy and eventually closed. The building was sold off and the site is now a block of flats.

Telford House, at the northern end of Clarence Street, was built in 1932 as Yeovil's new telephone exchange in the grounds of the white cottage seen on the right. The cottage was demolished in 1935 and Telford House was extended to the dimensions we see today, opening in 1936. Unusually, a datestone for the year of 1936 (when Edward VIII was briefly on the throne before his abdication) is on the wall of the extension facing Clarence Street.

Park Road Cottages were a long, two-storey, stone-built range that was originally outbuildings of Old Sarum House. The 1846 Tithe Apportionment noted that the cottages were owned by John Ryall Mayo. The window and door openings onto the street were probably later but the actual structures dated to the seventeenth century. Facing the interior yard and on the gable end were stone mullioned windows with drip moulds. The cottages were Grade III listed. They were, however, demolished (I believe) in the 1980s.

The Reformed Episcopalian Christ Church, on the left, together with a Sunday school building to its rear, was constructed in newly built Park Road and completed in 1880. Designed to seat a congregation of 500 and built in the Early English Revival style, it had a nave and chancel, a polygonal apse and a spirelet. However, the congregation of Christ Church dwindled dramatically and in 1904 the church fabric, together with the Sunday school building, were demolished. The church had lasted just twenty-five years.

In the 1860s, this building in Hendford, next to the Butchers Arms, was the photographic studios of early Yeovil photographer John Chaffin and, later, his children until 1919. It then became the Motor Mart Garage and petrol station for many years. Several occupiers followed, including the Yeovil Motor Cycle Mart during the 1960s, Moffat Marine in the 1970s and, finally, the Yeovil branch of the Women's Institute seen in this 1984 photograph shortly before its demolition.

Fielding House, Petters Way, was built in 1936 as the Yeovil Police Superintendent's house. To the right, off photo, was the new courts and police station building also of 1936. Further off photo to the left was the Baptist chapel. The police vacated the building in the early 1980s when the new police station opened in Horsey Lane and the building became occupied by solicitors Jeremy Wood & Co. Fielding House was demolished shortly after this photograph was taken. Today the site is occupied by a block of flats.

This car showroom, at the eastern end of Huish, backed onto Waterloo Lane and was opposite Douglas Seaton's car showroom on the corner of Huish and Clarence Street. At one time this was Seaton's second-hand car showrooms but at the time of this photograph, it was Yetminster Motor Co.'s showroom (named as such simply because the owner, Jeff Leach, lived in Yetminster).

The Crown Inn, in Huish, was operating as early as 1835, albeit not in this building, which appears to date from the 1880s. It was almost certainly owned and rebuilt by J Brutton & Sons as a tied house. The Crown Inn closed during the 1970s and for many years was used as the regional office for Bass Brewers. The building was demolished in 1991 as part of the Tesco redevelopment.

The building of a public swimming pool and baths in Yeovil was first suggested in 1876 but not approved by the council until 1883. Frequently known as the Corporation Baths, the new building was completed in 1885. Although enlarged and modernised more than once, the Huish pool was finally demolished in 1960, when it was rebuilt. The photograph here shows the new pool at the rear with part of the old pool, to the right, which housed the filtration and chlorination plant.

In 1846 a National Day School, the first of its kind in the area, was built in Huish. Intended for the education of poor children, for a penny a week they were taught reading, writing, arithmetic and needlework. However, in consequence of the very early age at which children were put to work at glove making, the school was initially 'very thinly attended'. The remaining school building, shown here, is now incorporated into the Tesco's building.

Castle Hotel, Middle Street, Yeovil.

Before its demolition in 1927 for street widening, the Castle Inn was Yeovil's earliest house. It was, in part, thirteenth century and had been an old medieval chantry property. When it first opened as licensed premises, probably before 1668, it was called the Hart or the White Hart. Later it was known as the Higher Three Cups or Upper Three Cups, until around 1750. The building had a fine arched doorway with Gothic-style hood moulding and stone mullioned windows.

The George Inn, Middle Street, seen here at left in the 1890s, began life as a private dwelling, built during the 1400s and from 1478 it was owned by the Trustees of the Woborn Almshouse. The last remaining secular medieval building in the town, the George was demolished for street widening in 1962. However, it transpired that the council did not own the land and the road couldn't be widened. Within ten years the road was pedestrianised, exposing the futility of the wanton destruction of this ancient piece of Yeovil's history.

Yeovil Town railway station opened in 1861 and a public house in Middle Street, facing Station Road, was named the Railway Inn. This building was demolished in 1913 when Central Road was built and a new Railway Tavern, seen in this photograph of around 1915, was built on the corner of Central Road. The Railway Tavern disappeared in the mid-1960s as part of the wholesale redevelopment of this part of Middle Street. The site is now Wetherspoon's William Dampier.

The Coronation Hotel and Vaults, facing the Triangle and seen here on left in a postcard of around 1910, opened in 1902. The building was demolished around 1965 as part of the Glovers Walk shopping complex. It had served Yeovil for only some fifty years before succumbing to the 'progress' of 1960s concrete and steel architecture – unfortunate for such a grand building and what was surely the most architecturally impressive of Yeovil's watering holes.

The town gasworks, off Middle Street, were built by the Yeovil Gas & Coke Company and completed in 1833 on the site of a drained withy bed. The enterprise was eventually acquired by the Corporation itself, under a local Act of Parliament in 1899. The gasworks closed in 1957 and the site was cleared in the early 1970s. The building seen here survives, albeit cosmetically altered, and until recently was an outlet of St Margaret's Hospice.

The town gasworks was complete with retorts and gasholders, as seen in this 1960s photograph taken from the western side of Stars Lane. By 1856 it was producing 28,000 cubic feet of gas daily and supplied gas to the Corporation's 124 street lamps. The town's gas supply continued to illuminate Yeovil until the close of the Second World War.

In 1849 a new Town Hall was built in High Street and behind it were built a Corn Exchange, a Meat Market and a Cheese Market, the whole complex extending from High Street all the way to South Street. In 1913 the fire service moved into the old Cheese Market building in South Street, opposite Petters Way and seen in this 1960s photograph. This building remained the fire station until its demolition in May 1961 when the new fire station in Reckleford was built in 1962.

The South Street National School was built as a Church of England infant and Sunday school and opened in 1860. It was built in South Street, facing the junction of Union Street, and was intended for children of the Holy Trinity (Hendford) parish. It became Yeovil's second National School with accommodation for 190 children. The school buildings were demolished in 1965.

Yeovil Town station, opened in 1861, was a joint station built by the London & South Western Railways Company (L&SWR) and the Great Western Railway Company (GWR). For many years Yeovil Town station was well known for having two station masters, one for each of the railway companies operating through it. This postcard from Summerhouse Hill, overlooking the Yeovil Town railway station, dates to 1905.

The first of Yeovil's stations to go was Hendford Halt, which closed in 1964, along with the line to Taunton. Next, Yeovil Town station (seen here in a postcard of 1919) closed to passenger traffic on 3 October 1966 but freight and parcels traffic continued to use the station until 9 October 1967 when these services were also withdrawn. Today the site of Yeovil Town station is covered by the Yeo Leisure Centre and its car park.

Victoria Buildings was a long row of cheap housing for leather and glove workers. It was named for Queen Victoria and was built, around the time of her accession in 1837, at the bottom of the western slope of Summerhouse Hill. Indeed, in the 1841 census, Victoria Buildings was referred to as 'New Walk' as well as its other local name of 'Heaven' by which the area was known for decades. This 1960s photograph shows the terrace on the far side of the railway line.

When the railway was built along the southern and western flanks of Summerhouse Hill in the 1860s, road access to Victoria Buildings was cut and necessitated the building of a bridge. Consequently, Victoria Bridge was built in the 1860s to carry the spur of Addlewell Lane over the newly built railway line to give continued road access to Victoria Buildings. Victoria Buildings were demolished in 1965 and the bridge was removed later, around 1977, and the road restored to its original level.

In 1913, a young Albert Percy Winsor, known as Percy, set himself up as an 'Implement Agent'. As his business grew, he established Percy Winsor Ltd, sellers of agricultural machinery. During the 1930s, he built the new art deco-influenced showrooms of this photograph at the western end of Vicarage Street. By the time of this 1940s photograph, the old Unitarian church next to the new building had been acquired by Percy, who adapted it for his use. All these buildings were demolished in the 1970s.

This Vicarage Street building, which housed the Army & Navy Stores, was built in 1890 by the Crewkerne United Breweries to replace their outlet for wines, spirits and ales already in Vicarage Street. The premises were put up for let in 1904 and the Army & Navy Stores, founded in 1871, later moved into the premises. In 1971, the Army & Navy Stores relocated to Glovers Walk and the Vicarage Street building was demolished in the 1980s.

This building, on the corner of Gordon Road and Mount Pleasant, was built in 1912. In the 1930s it was a grocery of the Yeovil & District Co-operative Society. It later became a Co-op butchery. Later still it became Eason's butchers. The building lay derelict for some ten years and was finally demolished in the early 2010s. Today the site contains a block of flats.

Around the turn of the century, Aplin & Barrett acquired some 2 acres of land on the eastern side of Newton Road, near its junction with Middle Street, that had been the extensive grounds of Osborne House. The Newton Road elevation of Aplin & Barrett's factory, producing dairy and meat products, is seen here shortly before demolition began in 1983. The site is now occupied by the flats of Ivel Court.

L. H. Nichols Ltd was a company of leather dressers and glove manufacturers, originally with their main production premises in Brunswick Street. The company moved to the Nautilus Works, Reckleford, around 1990. In 2013, with the end of the lease on the Yeovil factory and the retirement of key staff, the production transferred to New Zealand, trading as Nichols (New Zealand) Ltd. The Nichols' factory in Reckleford, photographed above, was demolished and the site cleared during the summer of 2015.

Pen Mill was one of the two Yeovil mills mentioned in the Domesday Book of 1086 – a mill valued at five shillings, which was almost certainly the predecessor of Pen Mill. In 1255 the Feet of Fines recorded 'Roger atte Penmalne' and in 1337 a reference was made to 'William de Penmull'. By the time of Snell's Directory of 1954–55, B. Chudleigh & Sons were listed as 'Millers & Corn Merchants of Hendford and Pen Mills'. Today the mill is no longer functioning.

Ashley's of Yeovil Ltd in West Hendford, seen here in 2003, was a precision engineering company carrying out work for the aerospace, motorsport, tobacco, medical and pharmaceutical industries. In 2008 planning consent was granted for a new Lidl food store to be built on the site. The former engineering works were demolished and the new supermarket opened in 2014.

The Yeovil and District Co-operative Society was founded in 1889, initially with just fifty members. Premises for a Co-operative Society grocery were found at a shop in Middle Street and in 1890 the society started a bakery. The society grew such that by 1937 there were nine branches in the district, four draperies, four gent's outfitters and shoe shops, two furniture outlets, a ladies' hairdressers, a confectionary, coal wharf, and a dairy in Grass Royal (seen here in 1998).

This two-page spread gives views of a further group of light industrial units, now long gone. Auto & General Electrical Services, of Goldcroft, was incorporated in 1954 and was originally based in Park Road. This view of the Goldcroft premises dates to 1998, shortly before the company was dissolved. This building was demolished and the site is now housing.

This nondescript light industrial unit sat largely unnoticed for many years towards the eastern end of South Street. The box factory was at one time the Somerset & Dorset Box Factory, latterly simply S&D, and at the time of this 2001 photograph, it was the premises of Cartons Ltd. Shortly after this photograph was taken, the building was demolished for a car park, appropriately known as the Box Factory car park.

The Southern Electricity Board was created in 1948 as part of the nationalisation of the electricity industry by the Electricity Act 1947. Yeovil District of the SEB was formed in 1949 by amalgamating Wessex Electricity Company's three districts of Yeovil, Frome and Shaftesbury. During the night of 2 August 1949, the Dampier Street stores originally belonging to the Wessex Electricity Company suffered a devastating fire. This was influential on the decision to build the new offices and stores at West Hendford.

The Vita-Ray Laundry was sited on the lower slopes of Wyndham Hill adjacent to the Sherborne Road and facing the junction with Lyde Road. The laundry opened in September 1930 but, by the time of this 1978 photograph, taken from Wyndham Hill, the laundry had closed. The buildings were later demolished and the site is now the small Wyndham View housing estate.

This King's Arms, in South Street, was a Yeovil beerhouse (meaning it wasn't licensed to sell spirits) and was run by Richard Bennetts. It was a very short-lived establishment, as it only appears in the records for a little over a decade. The building was completely destroyed by fire on 23 February 1906 as seen in this photograph by William Ross. The site of the King's Arms is now the rear loading area of the Argos store.

The original Bell Inn on this site in Preston Plucknett, surrounded by orchards, may have existed for generations before it was documented and at this time Preston Plucknett was just outside the Yeovil borough boundary. The Bell Inn was first named as such in Kelly's Directory of 1842. It was built of stone and had petrol pumps in the front. The Bell Inn was demolished for road widening in the late 1930s and replaced by a new pub of the same name.

A very late nineteenth-century public house, the Great Western in Camborne Grove was built to serve travellers using Pen Mill railway station (better thirty years late than never) and the local domestic market of Camborne Grove, Camborne Place and Camborne Street. It was, for its first year or so, known as the Camborne Inn. Seen here in 2012, the Great Western closed in 2017 and has since been converted into flats.

The Duke of Wellington, in Townsend, was operating as a beerhouse by 1869, at which time it was adjoining a private house called Medina Cottage, which later (after 1881) became part of the public house. Judging by its proximity to the Royal Osborne Brewery, it almost certainly was a tied house of that brewery. By 1991 the Duke of Wellington had closed and it was demolished the following year. The site is now a car park.

Tabernacle Lane has been known as such since the founding of the Calvinist Tabernacle Meeting House there in 1804. Built with seating for 400, the ecclesiastic census of 1851 recorded regular congregations of between 150 and 200. However, the congregation gradually dwindled and by the early twentieth century was quite small. Services finally ceased in 1920 and the Tabernacle building itself, seen as the gabled building to the right of the people in this photograph of the 1960s, was demolished in 1971.

A breakaway sect of Wesleyan Methodists founded the Primitive Methodists in New Town during the 1860s and built this chapel in South Street in 1865. The building could accommodate a congregation of 300. The Primitive Methodists reunited with the Wesleyans in 1932, and this same year the chapel ceased to be used as a place of worship, becoming a glove factory. In 1996, during alteration works, the front of the building collapsed and it had to be demolished. The site is now a car park.

An Elim Church began in 1928 at West Camel but moved to Yeovil the following year. A new sectional building was erected in Southville, opening in 1929. In 1962 the building was clad in brickwork, seen here, and a two-storey extension was added. In 1986 the whole building was demolished, to be replaced with a new building with the main entrance in Southville. The new building was officially opened by Paddy Ashdown on 28 November 1987.

In 1903 a building in the Avenue was acquired, together with the adjoining property, by the Sisters of St Gildas-des-Bois, who originated in Brittany, France. They built the St Gildas convent on the site. The Sisters envisaged their presence in Yeovil as a missionary one with education as a priority and, as a consequence, in September 1907 they opened a boarding and day school. The convent closed and was demolished in 1984. A sheltered housing scheme was built on the site in 1988.

During the 1990s many supermarkets began operating petrol filling stations. Sadly, this caused the demise of many small, local filling stations. This photograph shows the filling station on Hendford Hill, which closed in 2003 and is representative of several filling stations that were forced to close. These included filling stations in South Street, Market Street, Huish, West Hendford and St Michael's Avenue.

Originally Horsey Lane included, until the mid-nineteenth century, today's West Hendford and ran from its entrance opposite the Three Choughs in Hendford to the present junction of West Hendford and Beer Street, before turning sharply left to Hendford Bridge by today's Railway Hotel. The eastern side of today's Horsey Lane had housing built in the 1930s and the police station was built in the 1980s. The western side, now housing, has had a variety of businesses including a garage, a DIY store and this oil depot photographed in the 1980s.

The new twenty-bed Fiveways Hospital was built in 1871 and opened in January 1872, just as an outbreak of smallpox hit Yeovil. In 1916 the hospital trustees purchased Kingston Manor together with its extensive grounds, with the intention of building a new larger general hospital. When the new hospital opened in 1923, Fiveways Hospital became the new Maternity Unit. In 1968 a new maternity unit opened and Fiveways became redundant. The Fiveways Hospital was finally demolished in 1969.

By the time of the First World War, it was becoming clear that the Fiveways Hospital was too small for its purpose. The new General Hospital, with its entrance in Higher Kingston, opened in 1922. The new hospital was officially opened on 19 July 1923 by HRH the Prince of Wales, later Edward VIII. Ultimately, by the 1960s, the hospital was proving to be inadequate to meet the modern demands of the growing town. It was finally replaced by the present District Hospital in 1973.

This white tin hut was St Andrew's Hall, standing on the corner of Preston Grove and Grove Avenue, photographed in the 1980s. The hall was very popular and used for a great range of activities including Sunday school, play school, an overfill classroom for Summerleaze Park school, cubs, scouts, brownies and guides, discos and jumble sales. It now has a brick-built replacement.

Holy Trinity Hall, built of green-painted 'wriggly tin', was located on the corner of Mill Lane and Addlewell Lane for decades. As with St Andrew's Hall above, Holy Trinity hall was used by cubs, scouts, brownies, guides, and so on, as well as judo and karate. But, to the 'baby boomer' generation of Yeovilians, it will always be remembered as the Tuesday night 'Teen Beat' disco with regular live bands. The hall was demolished in 2000 and affordable flats were built on the site.

During the 1930s with the continual expansion of the town, it was not possible to gravity-feed a water supply to properties in the area of the Hundredstone Corner on Mudford Road. Because this is the highest point in Yeovil, it was necessary to pump water to a bulk water tank in Ashford Grove, then gravity-feed to the new local homes. The water tower was a clear skyline landmark visible, for instance, from the A303 5 miles to the north. The water tank was demolished, as seen here, in 2005.

Houndstone Camp was a permanent Second World War military camp used extensively by the British Army, although in 1942 the British garrisons moved out of the Yeovil army camps in order to make way for incoming Americans. Houndstone was home to several American units and became their 9th Replacement Depot and the US Army's 169th General Hospital. 110 men of the Czechoslovak Independent Brigade and 138 men of the Reconnaissance Section were also billeted here. Today Houndstone Camp has all but disappeared.

Yeovil solicitor Thomas Moore's home and legal practice, 'Far End House' in Higher Kingston, was built during the 1830s. Its large, impressive gardens swept all the way down to Kingston but the back of the house was located directly onto Higher Kingston. In 1961, Far End House was owned by the Ministry of Health but lay empty for several years – as seen in this photograph. The house was demolished in the late 1960s.

Kingston Manor House was an early Georgian house of two storeys and six bays with a Tuscan porch. In a lease of 1801 it was described as a 'Capital Mansion House in Yeovil … with coach house, stables, offices, courtyard, gardens, orchard and paddock containing 6 acres…' The house itself was sold and became a nursing home attached to the new Yeovil General Hospital in 1916. Kingston Manor House was demolished for the building of Yeovil District Hospital in the 1970s.

South Street House was a large Georgian town house, being shown on all the early maps of Yeovil from Watts' map of 1806 onwards. It was of six bays and two storeys, fronting directly onto South Street. It had a large rear garden. For many years it was the home and medical practice of Dr Ptolemy Colmer, later mayor of Yeovil. The house was demolished and the site is now the car park alongside the entrance to Petters Way.

This image dates to 1909, with the sign reading 'Yeovil County School for Boys'. The building to the left is the extension to the school built in the period between 1883 and 1892 by John Aldridge. To the right is the original three-storey house in which he founded Kingston School. The house had been built prior to 1831. Following the school's move to Mudford Road, the original Kingston School building was demolished in 1968.

Built in the 1820s, Brunswick Street runs from Hendford as far as the junction of Penn Hill, after which the road was named Belmont and then became Park Street. In 1825 'the new road belonging to Peter Daniell' was referenced in a marriage settlement. This was a new road which, combined with Park Street running from the east, replaced the circuitous and somewhat steep route of Addlewell Lane and Chant's Path. The road was originally known as New France, later France Street. This image dates to 1906.

In the late 1820s or early 1830s, Peter Daniell planned and built an extension to Grope Lane (today's Wine Street), which became Union Street. He built Bond Street, to connect Middle Street with South Street, possibly as early as 1824. Finally, Peter Daniell constructed Peter Street, named after himself, to join Bond Street with Grope Lane/Union Street. The initials 'PL PD' and the date 1836 were formerly on one of these original houses in the street, seen here in a 1960s photograph.

Originally known as Frogg Lane or Frogg Street, Park Street was laid out and built by Peter Daniell between 1825 and 1834 along the edge of his Penn House estate. During the nineteenth century, Park Street/Belmont/Brunswick Street acquired an unsavoury reputation primarily because it had nine named pubs and a minimum of an additional six beerhouses – a total of fifteen drinking establishments. Almost all the buildings in Park Street were demolished in the 1960s.

Although mostly incorporated within Yeovil in 1928 (small parts being absorbed by the adjacent parishes of Brympton and West Coker), Preston Plucknett retained a rural village charm. Its many thatched roadside cottages survived until the 1960s when the majority of the cottages on either side of Preston Road were demolished for road widening and straightening. This photograph, of around 1965, was taken just before these cottages were demolished.

Lost Interiors

This is the grand staircase of Hendford Manor, photographed in the late 1970s. Having been left to the ravages of wet and dry rot, the house (apart from the external walls and the roof) was completely gutted inside shortly after this photograph.

Originally built as a small town house, the Fleur-de-Lys was a two-storied and cellared brick building at the location now occupied by Beales in High Street. The Fleur-de-Lys had been a public house at least since the mid-eighteenth century, or probably much earlier still. It was also known as the Plume of Feathers. This is a photograph taken in the old rediscovered cellars of the Fleur-de-Lys in 1934 – about the time it ceased trading.

Borough House was originally an eighteenth-century house in High Street. Borough House was purchased by Yeovil Corporation in 1898 to be used as the town's first municipal offices. The building served as a council chamber and offices until it was demolished in 1924 for the new development of King George Street. This photograph, of the council chamber, was taken around 1915. The photographs on the wall were of members of the Corporation. These were taken and presented by Jarratt Beckett, photographer of Hendford.

THE GREEN LANTERN
RESTAURANT
YEOVIL · PHONE 74

The Green Lantern was a short-lived restaurant in Kingston during the latter part of the 1940s in what had been a private house. All references to the restaurant, which could accommodate up to 150 persons, date to between 1947 and 1950 – the date of this advertising postcard. It was reported several times as the venue for the annual dinners of various Yeovil societies and organisations. Note its telephone number – Yeovil 74.

The first public showing of a film in Yeovil was at the Assembly Rooms in Princes Street in 1896 and the Central Auction Rooms in Church Street followed in 1912. In May 1930, a fire broke out in the cinema, causing such extensive damage that a complete rebuild was necessary. The rebuilt Central Cinema opened in January 1932. This photograph, glimpsing the decorative barrel ceiling and the opulent end wall above the screen, was taken at the time of demolition in 1983.

74

By 1875, William Frederick Banfield started a bakery in Middle Street. He advertised himself as a 'Cook, Confectioner, Fancy Bread and Biscuit Baker' in the *Western Gazette* and within a year or two was advertising in *Whitby's Yeovil Almanack Advertiser* as a baker, wholesale and retail confectioner and caterer for wedding parties, etc. In 1928 he moved to the Cottage Café premises (seen above and below) and this 1930's photograph shows the bakery he created behind the café.

The building that housed the Cottage Café in Hendford probably dates to the eighteenth century and was built as a small town house. In 1928 William Banfield opened the Cottage Café in the premises. At the rear of the premises, he built a bakery. With kitchens on both floors, the ground floor had a café as well as a shop, while upstairs boasted a large dining room, seen in this photograph of the 1960s. The Cottage Café closed in 1972.

This photograph, taken in pre-health and safety days around 1910, is of Hayne's butcher's shop in the Borough (literally). In 1890 John Coombs Hayne moved his family to Yeovil and took over his brother's butcher's business. After his death in 1924, the business was carried on by John's son Sidney. The business moved from the Borough to its present location at the northern end of Princes Street in 1939.

During the 1840s livestock auctioneer William Gifford Palmer came to Yeovil. He acquired premises on the corner of Court Ash and Market Street, together with gardens and orchards behind, where he established his new cattle market, probably in 1852. The 3.7-acre Yeovil cattle market closed in 2008 and has lain derelict ever since. This photograph, of around 1985, shows covered sheep pens in the market.

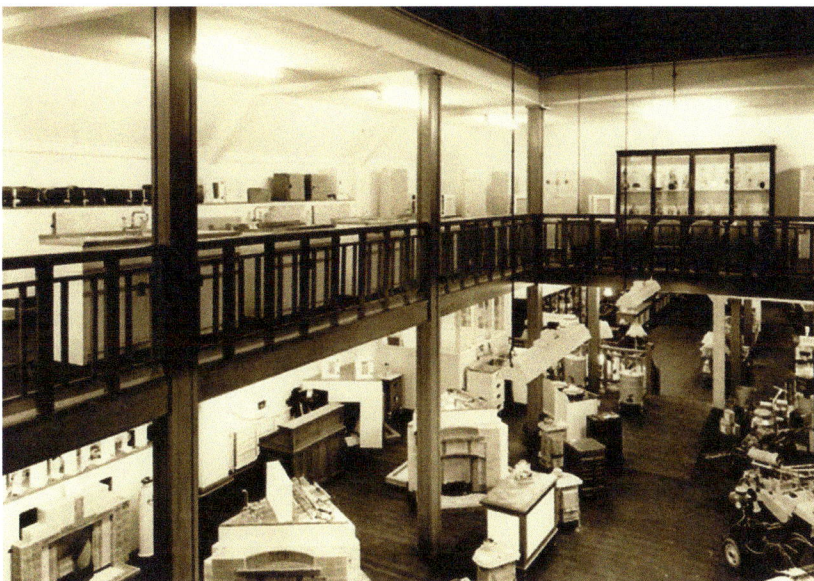

During the 1890s two young lads, Harry Hill and John Sawtell, both worked for James Petter as assistants in the ironmongery side of Petter's many business interests. With the retirement of James Petter, his sons reorganised the company. The ironmongery business was then formed into a company under the name of Hill, Sawtell & Co., in which the Petter family held the principal interest. This 1940 photograph shows the interior of the shop in the Borough, which is now Superdrug.

Thomas Jesty had acquired some of his father's carpentry skills and in the 1881 census, he was listed as an 'Undertaker & Furniture Dealer' of the Triangle (recently the site of Poundland), which he called his 'Furniture Warehouse' – seen in this 1906 photograph. Thomas died in 1904, and the business was renamed Jesty & Co. after his death. It was then run by his widow Sarah and her son by her first marriage, William Stevens, who was to run the business until at least 1965.

Seen here in a photograph of 2010, the Picketty Witch pub had nothing to do with witches. In fact, the name comes from the Old English 'piccede' meaning a 'triangular or pointed piece of land' and 'wice' being a Wych Elm that would, at one time, been a noticeable landmark of the area. The pub was built in the 1930s to serve the rapidly expanding housing in the vicinity. The Picketty Witch finally closed in late 2012 and was converted into a Tesco Express.

The Great Western, in Camborne Grove, was a very late nineteenth-century public house, built to serve travellers using Pen Mill railway station and the local domestic market of Camborne Grove, Camborne Place and Camborne Street. It was, for its first year or so, known as the Camborne Inn. This photograph was taken during the summer of 2017 and the Great Western closed its doors on 2 December 2017. It is currently being converted into flats.

The Yeovil Corporation Baths in Huish, affectionately known by many older Yeovilians as the 'old Pool', opened in October 1885. Of course, at this time, swimming sessions of men and women were strictly segregated; propriety apart, the poolside changing accommodation was one of the chief problems. Separate sessions for men and women were adopted from the start. Although enlarged and modernised more than once, the Huish pool was finally demolished in 1960. This photograph, of around 1908, shows boys from Kingston School receiving swimming lessons.

The 'new' Huish swimming pool, which replaced the 'old' pool (above), opened in 1962. The pool had tiered spectator seating along the western side. The depth of 12.5 feet at one end allowed diving stages of one 5-metre firm board and a 3-metre and 1-metre springboards. In 1992, this pool was replaced by the Goldenstones Pools & Leisure Centre.

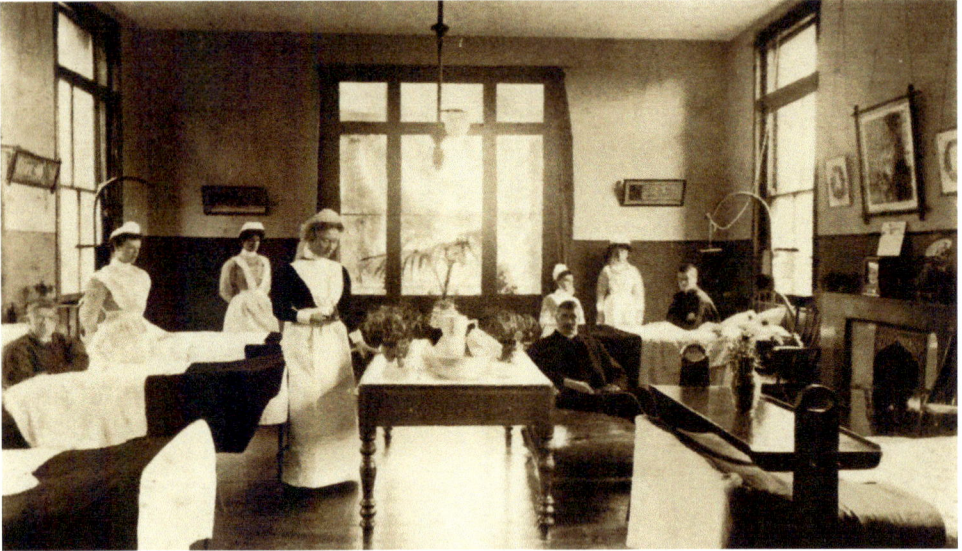

The Yeovil General Dispensary, a precursor to later Yeovil hospitals, was instituted in 1858 in Kingston. However, by the mid-1860s, it was clear that the dispensary was rapidly outgrowing the facilities. Consequently, the new twenty-bed Fiveways Hospital was built at a cost of £1,195 (around £630,000 in today's value). The hospital opened in January 1872 just as an outbreak of smallpox hit Yeovil. This photograph, of 1909, shows the matron, several nurses and patients in the men's ward at the Fiveways Hospital.

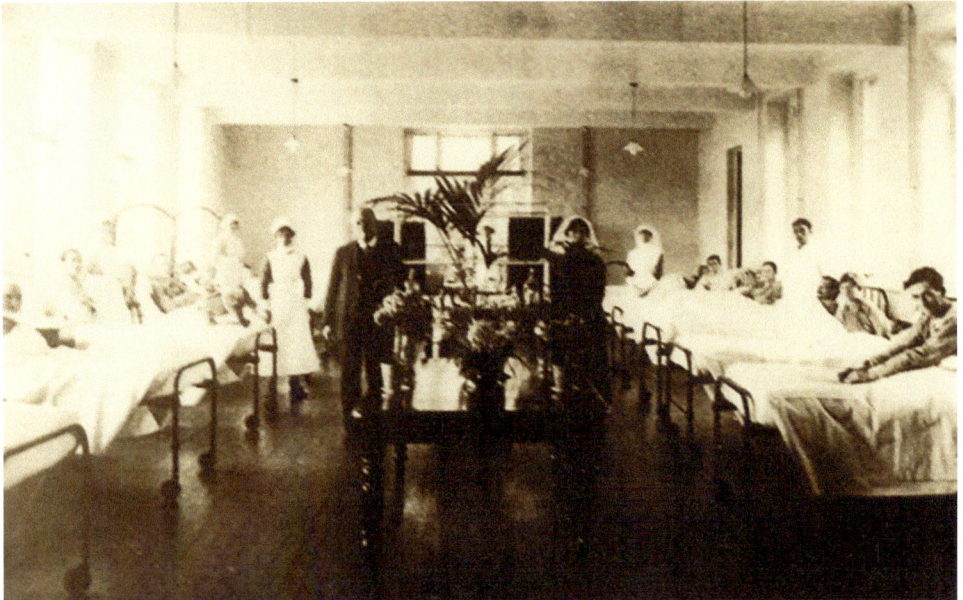

By the time of the First World War, it was becoming clear that the Fiveways Hospital was too small for its purpose. In 1916 the hospital trustees purchased Kingston Manor, together with its extensive grounds known as Bide's Gardens, with the intention of building a new larger general hospital. Because of the war, building on the new hospital site did not begin until 1921. This is a photograph of the men's ward in the new General Hospital, shortly after it opened in 1923.

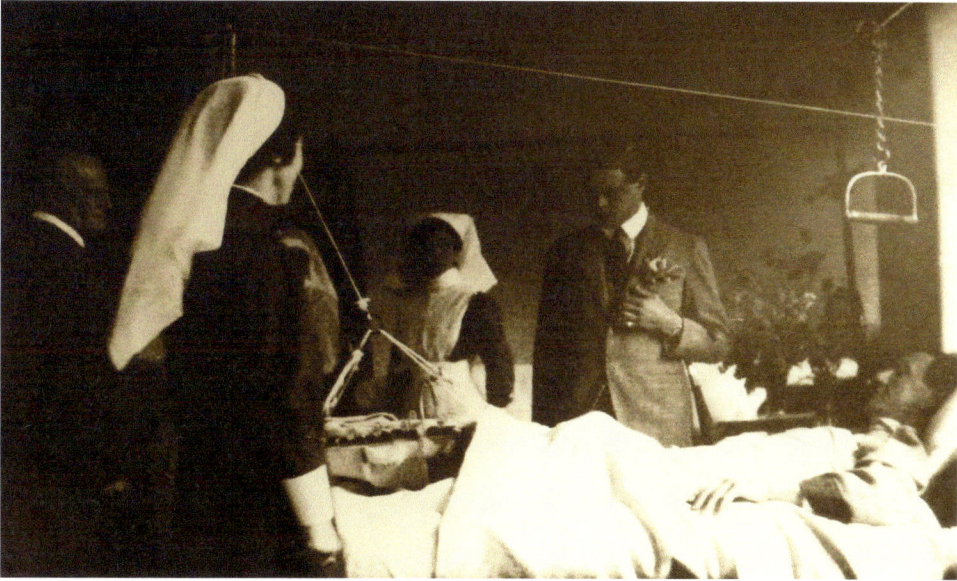

The General Hospital featured electrical lighting and full central heating throughout. The building, with its entrance in Higher Kingston, cost over £20,000 (around £3.5 million in today's value) to build. The new General Hospital opened, and the first patients were admitted, on 16 December 1922. The hospital was officially opened on 19 July 1923 by HRH the Prince of Wales, later Edward VIII, seen here.

X-rays were only discovered in 1896, and in 1916 the Yeovil X-ray Fund was begun in order to raise funds for a new X-ray machine for Fiveways Hospital. The fund continued into 1917 and, eventually, enough money was raised to buy Yeovil's first X-ray machine. This is a photograph of the 1930s, showing the X-ray Department at Yeovil General Hospital.

Yeovil's Watch House, the early equivalent of a police station, was originally in the Tolle Hall in the Borough but by the 1830s had literally been falling down for years. In 1849 the Town Commissioners commissioned a new building in Union Street to replace the decrepit Tolle Hall. Known as the Town House, it was a police station and also the residence for the Superintendent. The original police station cells, seen here, are today entered from the Mayor's Parlour.

The new 1932 telephone exchange, Telford House, was originally T-shaped in plan with a three-bay elevation to Clarence Street. It was extended during 1935–36 and is marked with a scarce datestone for the year of 1936 when Edward VIII was briefly on the throne before his abdication. In 1972–73, the new GPO sorting office in Huish was built and became the new home of the Yeovil telephone exchange. This photograph, of 1939, shows new telephone exchange equipment in Telford House.

Yeovil High School for Girls was founded in 1891, initially with just a dozen pupils. The school grew rapidly, and a new school building opened in The Park in 1896. In 1946, Park Lodge was acquired and adapted as an annexe to the High School. In 1945, it became a fully maintained state school and at this time the school had 252 pupils. This photograph, of 1954, shows the General Certificate cookery class.

The Sisters of St Gildas-des-Bois, who originated in Brittany, France, built a convent in Yeovil in 1903. The Sisters envisaged their presence here as one of education and, consequently, in September 1907 they opened a boarding and day school. It was run by the nuns, the Sisters of Christian Instruction, as a private school. Today, although the convent closed and the nuns moved away in 1984, St Gildas' School remains. This 1930s postcard shows a dormitory in the school.

Lost Trades

The street sweeper has long since traded a broom for an electrically motorised sweeper.

Yeovil clay was suitable for brick making and the soft, bright-red bricks are found everywhere in the older parts of the town. The main Yeovil brickworks were located north of Reckleford. Extensive brickworks were also to be found at St Michael's Avenue, originally known as Brickyard Lane. There were several other, smaller brickworks in the town such as at New Town, Preston Road and Ilchester Road. Most of the Yeovil brick-making sites were small in scale and didn't last for long.

Making rope and twine, and the associated trades of manufacturing webbing and sacking was established centuries ago in Yeovil and continued into the twentieth century. John Neal, a ropemaker but also recorded as a 'sack, sacking & twine manufacturer', had a ropeworks in Reckleford, opposite Goldcroft. Other Yeovil ropewalks were located at Fair Ground, between North Lane and Court Ash, with another running alongside the eastern edge of Mount Pleasant. Roping Road had been the site of an eighteenth-century rope and twine works.

Until the middle of the twentieth century, it was not unusual to see independent traders pushing handcarts around the streets of Yeovil to sell their wares. Largely due to the introduction of electric milk floats and supermarkets in the 1960s, milk deliveries made by the likes of J. White (in this photograph), pushing handcarts became a thing of the past. This two-page spread features some trades that have all but disappeared.

Ben Thorne became a familiar sight around Yeovil with his knife and scissor grinding machine. For years he would push his little handcart around the town and sharpen blades of all descriptions for both companies and individuals. Apart from knife grinding, he fixed pots, pans, china, glass and even mended umbrellas. His daughter recalled 'He used to sharpen the blades for the gloving scissors at the gloving factories. He also used to sharpen the blade on a lawnmower for just two shillings.'

John Bower was a sometime labourer and was often in trouble with the police, even spending six weeks in the cells of the police station in Union Street. In this photograph, taken in 1926, John Bower and his son Charles were working as chimney sweeps – yet another trade not often encountered in these days of centrally heated homes – based at their home at No. 103 Park Street. In the photograph, Charles is seen wearing two medals from his service in the First World War.

During the latter half of the nineteenth century, Yeovil had three small, independent aerated water manufacturers and bottlers: Vincent's Mineral Water Manufactory at the rear of the Royal Osborne brewery, the Yeovil Mineral and Aerated Water Works in Union Street and Channing's steam-powered aerated water manufactory. Channing's was bought by Henry Trask in 1891 and the aerated water business was carried on by Henry's descendants until at least 1954. This 1920s photograph shows Trask's office and factory in Vicarage Street.

This two-page spread features the firm of Aplin & Barrett of Newton Road. Founded in 1888, Aplin & Barrett became famous for their cheese and dairy products, which, from 1901, traded under the St Ivel brand. The 1936 photographs on these pages, however, feature their lesser-known meat and fish products. This photograph shows the preparing room, where raw materials were weighed out, passed twice through mincing machines and through a battery of Premier mills seen on the left.

This photograph shows the filling room, where small glass pots were filled with meat or fish pastes. The pots were filled by a girl at one end of a stainless steel table equipped with a travelling belt. Succeeding girls levelled off the paste, wiped the rim of the glass pots, inserted the parchment circles, placed on the rings and caps, and finally deposited the pots in wire baskets together with metal labels giving the batch numbers.

This photograph shows the pie room. The pastry ingredients were weighed before being mixed by machine. Weighed amounts of the meat and eggs were then filled into the pie shells and the lids placed on. Baking was done in a bank of coke-fired ovens. After baking, the pies were tipped out of the tins and placed on wire trays, which were then conveyed through a cooling tunnel. Finally, the pies were packed into individual window cartons.

The sausage room, seen here, is where a range of Aplin & Barret sausages were produced. The meat received from the butcher's room was passed first through a cutter, then through two different mincers. The sausage meat was filled into casings in the usual way, then wiped, weighed and boxed. The photograph shows filling operations (left), followed by linking, weighing and boxing.

The final six pages of this book are devoted to what had been the mainstay of the town for generations – the leather and gloving industries. By the 1890s it has been estimated that between 70 and 80 per cent of the town's population were involved in the leather, gloving and associated industries. From the 1950s, the gloving industry fell into decline and the last of Yeovil's glove manufacturing companies closed in 1989. Leather production still remains. The following photographs show a host of related trades that have since been almost lost.

Both photographs on this page were taken in 1924 at the premises of leather dressers and glove manufacturers Blake & Fox. The upper photograph shows the leather-dressing yard where the men are working at the soaking and lime pits. The lower photograph shows the unhairing department, where skins were scraped free from flesh and hair before going on to the stretching process.

Both photographs on this page are of processes at L. H. Nichols, who specialised in producing slink lambskins. This photograph shows part of the degreasing process. After storage, the skins were 'degreased', which removed all the excess fat in the skin. After this, the skin was 'fleshed' on a fleshing machine to remove any remaining surplus fat. The skins would then be washed and excess water removed. The skins would then be tanned.

Tanning is the process of treating perishable raw skins and hides and converting them into leather. Tanning permanently alters the protein structure of skin, making it more durable and less susceptible to rot. After tanning, the skins might then be passed over a carborundum wheel to create a suede finish. The skins would next be placed in the large drum, seen here, to have a degree of fat liquor put back in to lubricate and soften them before drying.

Following the tanning process, the skins would be washed in a bath of alum and salt, and then dried either in the open air or in artificially heated rooms. When thoroughly free from moisture they were next bathed in the yolk of eggs, sorted and taken to the dying rooms. Here, the skins were dyed with various shades of colour. Often, up to thirty different dyes were used.

The following three images are again photographs of processes at L. H. Nichols Ltd. This particular photograph shows lamb skins being processed on a wet carborundum wheel. This operation further 'unhairs' the leather and produces a fine suede finish. Rather than being a special leather, the term suede refers to a particular finish of leather that gives the fabric a soft and warm effect.

The staking process makes leather softer by softening the leather fibres. A staking machine has two plates with raised knobs and opposing recesses. Constant vibration ensures the leather is pressed into the recesses by the knobs causing the fibre to stretch. This method stretches and softens the leather so that the total surface of the hide increases. Staking also reinforces the grain pattern and reduces looseness.

Suede is a type of leather with a napped (raised or 'fuzzy') finish, commonly used for gloves. The term comes from the French 'gants de Suède', which literally means 'gloves from Sweden'. This photograph shows the final stage of suede production in which a 'plush wheel' is used to raise the suede finish. From here, the leather enters the glove manufacturing process.

The initial stage of glove manufacturing is to size and grade the skins. Using a 'trank', or template, the worker grades the skins as one trank or two tranks. A trank forms the palm, back and fingers of the glove, therefore a two-trank skin would produce a pair of gloves. Offcuts would be used to produce thumbs, fourchettes (the inside panels on the fingers of some glove styles) and so on.

The cutter was the person who cut out the leather into the parts required to make a glove. Cutters were the most highly paid of all the various leather and gloving trades and Vickery noted in 1856 'The wages average, to cutters when fully employed, from 25s to 30s per week.' This compares with the average agricultural labourer's weekly wage of between 7s and 10s. This photograph, of around 1930, shows the cutting room at the Clothier & Giles factory.

Traditionally, gloves had been hand-sewn by outworkers; women and girls (often as young as six or seven) working in their own homes as a form of cottage industry. The invention of the gloving 'donkey' in 1807 revolutionised the gloving industry by allowing the stitcher to produce accurate hand stitching. By the end of the nineteenth century, however, the introduction of sewing machines brought sewing into the factory, as seen in this sewing machine room of around 1915.

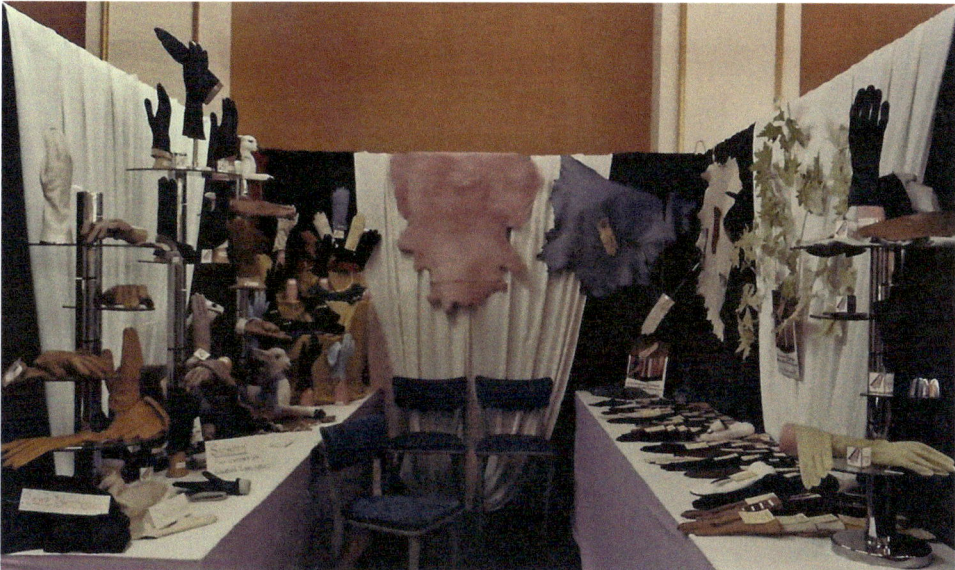

After the Second World War, the gloving industry in Yeovil went into rapid decline. In April 1989 the last of Yeovil's glove manufacturing companies, Freke & Gifford Ltd of Pen Mill Trading Estate, closed. The closure was blamed on cheap foreign imports, thereby ending a centuries-old craft industry that had made Yeovil internationally famous. This photograph shows the wide range of gloves manufactured by Denner & Vaughan on their exhibition stand at the 1965 British Glove Fair.

Acknowledgements

Many thanks to Mike Monk for proofreading not only this book but also my 2,100+ page website – www.yeovilhistory.info – which details in much greater depth every subject in this book. Many photographs in this book are from the author's collection, but the author and publisher would like to thank the following people for permission to use copyright material in this book: Rob Baker, Bob Banfield, Len Copland, John Cornelius, Roger Froude, Colin Haine, Allan Harding, Malcolm Nichols, Michael Ottewell, Jack Sweet and Brian Vaughan. Every attempt has been made to seek permission for copyright material used in this book. However, if we have inadvertently used copyright material without permission or acknowledgement we apologise and will make the necessary correction at the first opportunity.

About the Author

Local historian Bob Osborn is the author of nearly twenty books on an eclectic range of subjects. After a career in architecture, admin management, web design and management and, latterly, as a Learning Centre manager and Yeovil College lecturer teaching IT, he is now retired. Bob moved from North London to Yeovil, Somerset, in 1973 and since retiring works almost daily researching and compiling his ever-growing website 'The A-to-Z of Yeovil's History', which currently has over 10,000 images. Bob has four grown-up children and lives in Yeovil with his wife Carolyn and Alice the cat.

Bob's local history titles, published by Amberley, include *A–Z of Yeovil*, *Secret Yeovil*, *Yeovil in 50 Buildings*, *Now That's What I Call Yeovil* and *Yeovil from Old Photographs*.